Aircraft Marshalling Signals for Kids! Talking to Pilots! Technology for Kids

Children's Aviation Books

Copyright 2016

All Rights reserved. No part of this book may be reproduced or used in any way or form or by any means whether electronic or mechanical, this means that you cannot record or photocopy any material ideas or tips that are provided in this book

Have you seen those people doing signals on ramps when an airplane lands? Read on and learn about what these signals mean!

Marshalling is the exchange of visual signals between ground personnel and pilots.

The ground personnel giving the signals is called a marshaller. They usually wear a safety vest, a helmet and gloves. They hold marshalling bright-colored wands.

Marshallers signal the pilot to turn, slow down, stop and so on. These signals help the pilot maneuver the airplane to its designated parking slot.

When airplanes land at night, marshallers use illuminated wands so pilots can see their signals.

When parking, marshallers position themselves infront of the left wingtip so the pilot could see them with ease.

The next pages are the common marshalling signals.

HOLD/STAND BY

PLACE YOURSELF FACING ME

NORMAL STOP

TURN LEFT

TURN RIGHT

CHOCKS INSERTED

CHOCKS INSERTED

STOP ENGINES

START ENGINES

PROCEED

CHOCKS REMOVED

CHOCKS REMOVED

MOVE AHEAD

MOVE BACK

CONNECT TO GROUND POWER

DISCONNECT TO GROUND POWER

STRAIGHT AHEAD

SLOW DOWN

MOVE BACK

ALL CLEAR

NEGATIVE

ESTABLISH COMMUNICATION

Did you enjoy learning about the marshalling signals? Share this book with your friends!

www.ingramcontent.com/pod-product-compliance
Lightning Source LLC
LaVergne TN
LVHW061321060426
835507LV00019B/2252